I CAN SEE YOUR HOUSE FROM HERE!

ANOTHER BOOK OF INAPPROPRIATE HUMOR

BY STEVE CASE

THE APOCRYPHILE PRESS
BERKELEY, CA

apocryphile press
BERKELEY, CA

Apocryphile Press
1700 Shattuck Ave #81
Berkeley, CA 94709
www.apocryphile.org

Printed in the United States of America
ISBN 978-1-944769-27-7

And Introduction to the Second Volume

by the Archangel Gabriel

Okay remember last time when I was telling you about where Jesus got his sense of humor? Yeah, his mother was the funny one, but that kind of humor comes from somewhere deeper...maybe I should say higher.

God was laughing when he made the universe. He was a like a two-year-old who got into the finger paint. Most of the people he worked with along the way had a sense of humor...it was in the job description. How you people managed to screw all that I up I'll never know. Your somber preachers, your committees, your finger pointing, and oh the condemning. Let me tell you, you don't want to be in the workshop when those prayers start coming up.

It was a gift. All of it. All of creation was given unto you (I love that word "unto." We quit using that.) God gave you this universe as your playground. Then someone down there stood up (again probably in a committee meeting) and said, "Noooooooooooooo! You have to go to school! You have to get a job! You have to save all your money until you die. Oh and stop laughing, this is church for God's sake."

The Bible was full of jokesters, pranksters, smartasses, comedians, and fools.

People seemed to like the first book, so God asked me to troll the archives and come up with some of the best lines from the Old Testament. So here they are.

Oh and because someone said this a long time ago...let me say it here so you know.

You can laugh.

Yours,

Gabriel

Gabriel
Archangel/straight-man

The Bible was full of jokesters, pranksters, smartasses, comedians, and fools.

IN THE BEGINNING...
HEY UNIVERSE...HOWYADOIN'?
YOU KNOW AT FIRST I DIDN'T KNOW HOW TO CREATE THE SUN..
THEN IT DAWNED ON ME.

i can see your house from here

AWAKEN ADAM. I HAVE CREATED FOR YOU A WOMAN. SHE IS YOUR COMPANION, YOUR HELPMATE YOUR...
FIND ME THE REMOTE.

THE CREATORS OF THIS BOOK
WOULD LIKE TO REMIND READERS
OF THE WORD "INAPPROPRIATE" ON
THE FRONT COVER AND POINT OUT
THAT THIS JOKE WAS IN NO WAY
MEANT TO DISRESPECT WOMAN AND THIS
DISCLAMER WAS NOT INFFLUENCED
BY THE WRITERS WIFE. I LOVE YOU HONEY.

SERIOUSLY?

YEAH, WE DON'T ASK ALOT OF QUESTIONS AROUND HERE.

LOOK ADAM
I HAVE CREATED
YOU A WOMAN.
WILL YOU HAVE A DATE WITH ME?

NO. BUT I'D SHARE AN APPLE.

i can see your house from here

MOM! THINK DAD HAS LOST IT.
WHAT DO YOU MEAN?
HE KEEPS LICKING THE ANIMALS AND THEN MAKING NOTES.

HEY DAD, WHY DO SCUBA DIVERS FALL BACKWARD OUT OF THE BOAT?
WHY?
CAUSE IF THEY FELL FORWARD THEY'D STILL BE IN THE BOAT.

i can see your house from here

OKAY, ALL THOSE
IN FAVOR
OF LARRY FINDING
A NEW ROCK...

i can see your house from here

AND YOU WONDER WHY
THEY DIDN'T INCLUDE
YOUR NAME IN THE BIBLE

i can see your house from here

DANIEL, IF I LET YOU OUT WILL YOU RAN THROUGH THE CAMP SITE?
DON'T YOU MEAN "RUN". GOD?
NO, I MEAN "RAN"...

i can see your house from here

i can see your house from here

i can see your house from here

KNOW WHAT THEY SAY
ABOUT CLIFFHANGERS...

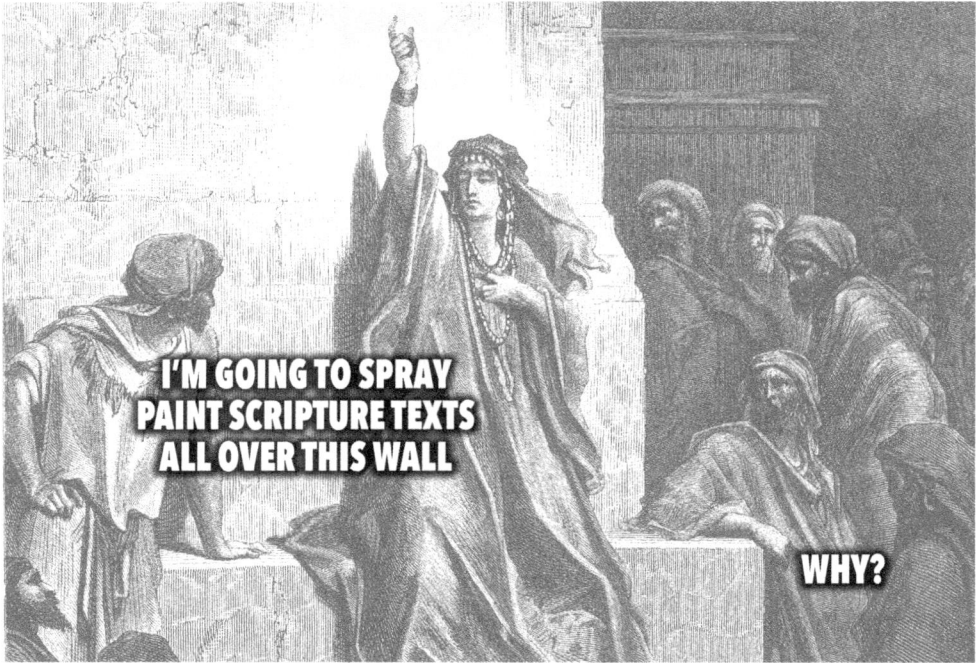

i can see your house from here

YOU'VE BEEN SITTING ON THAT ONE FOR A WHILE HAVEN'T YOU?

i can see your house from here

59

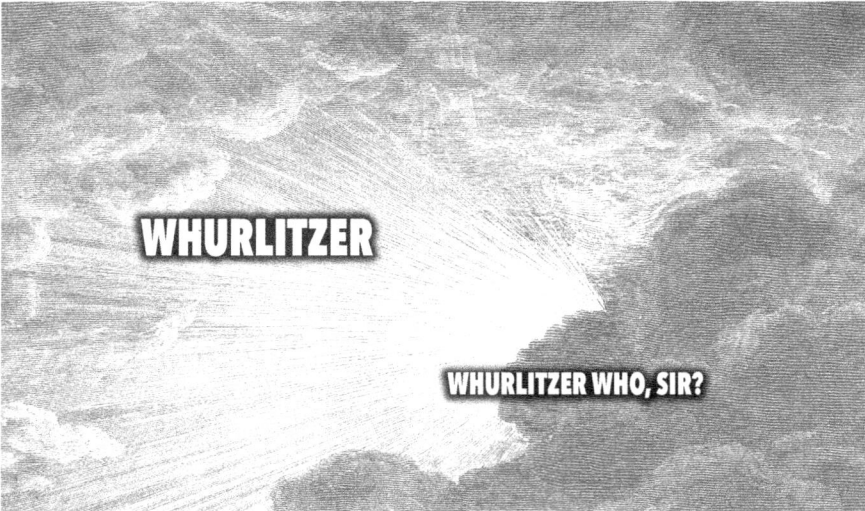

WHURLITZER ONE FOR THE MONEY...TWO FOR THE SHOW...
YOUR ELVIS IS IMPECCABLE, SIR.

i can see your house from here

69

i can see your house from here

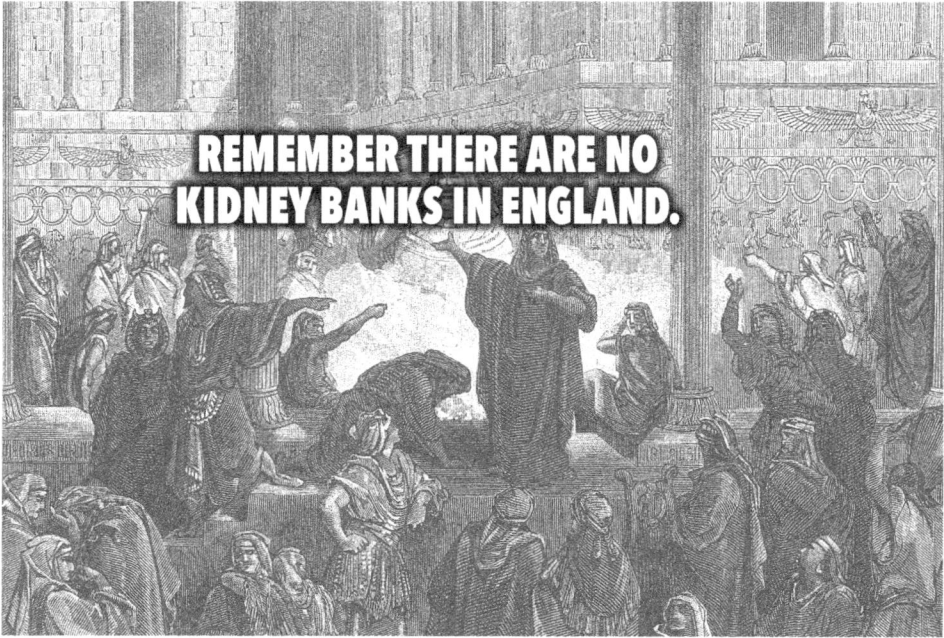

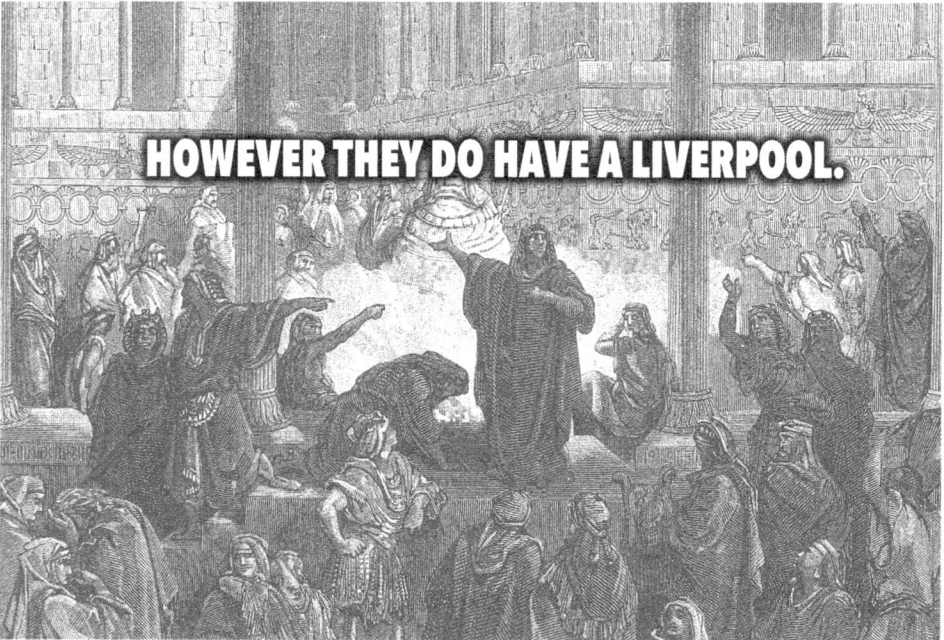

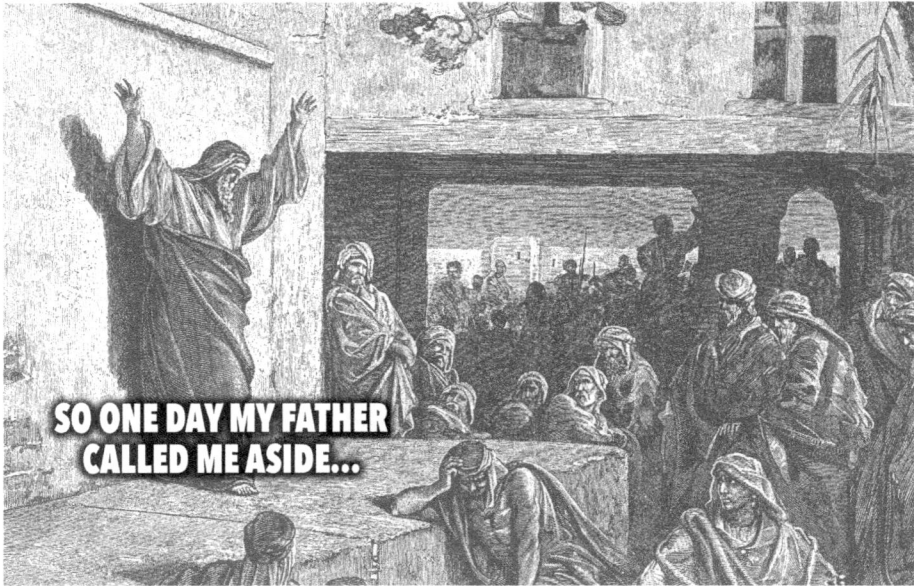

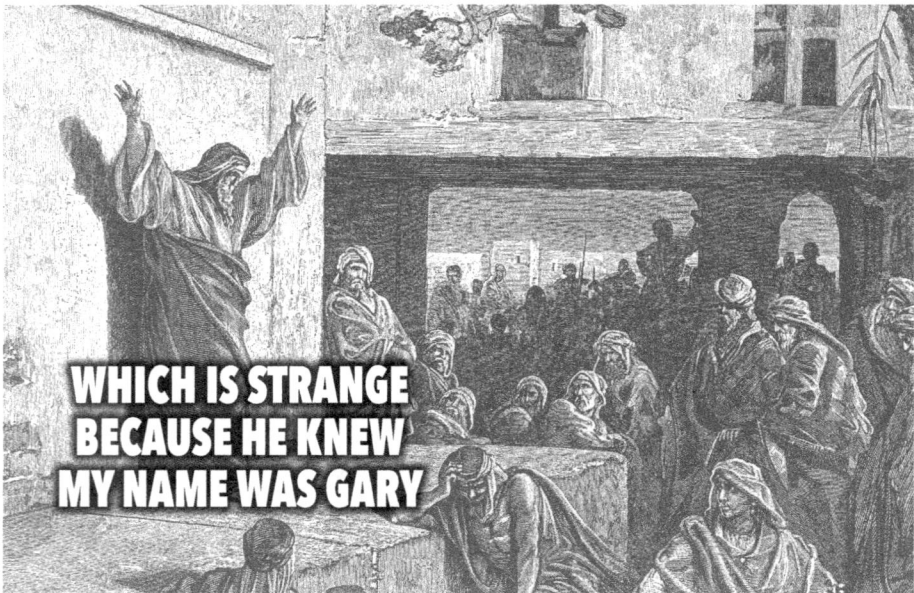

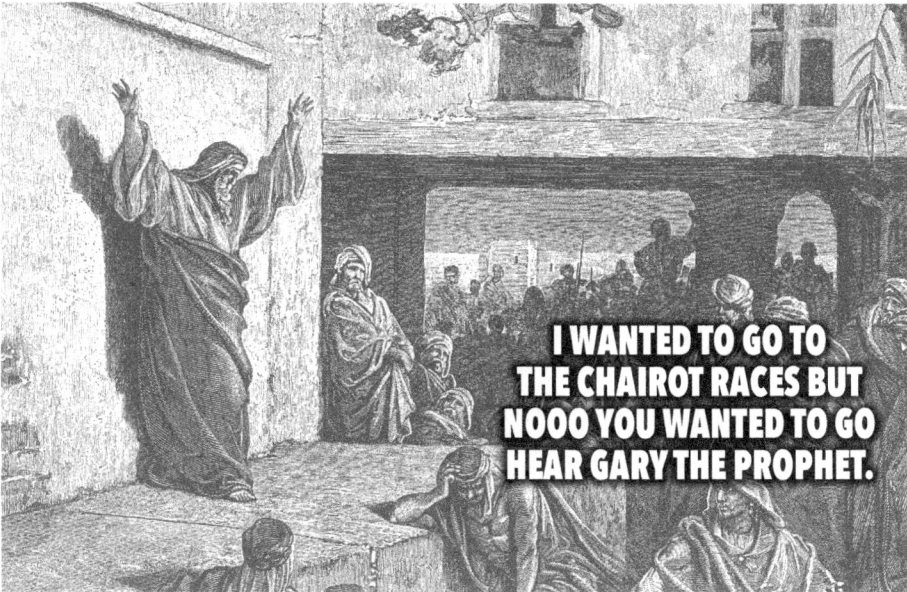

"TAP DANCE"

MY GRAND FATHER'S FAMILY RAN A DRY CLEANERS OVER IN JERUSALEM...
FIFTY YEARS ON THE SAME SPOT.
YOU WOULD HAVE THOUGHT THEY COULD HAVE CLEANED IT OUT BY NOW

NOW HERE'S
BUCK AND ROY
AND PICKIN'
AND GRINNIN'

i can see your house from here

i can see your house from here

BA-DUM TISHHHHHH

i can see your house from here

85

i can see your house from here

i can see your house from here

LEAVE ME ALONE, LARRY.

i can see your house from here

i can see your house from here

i can see your house from here

93

i can see your house from here

ALL HAIL THOUS BLESSED VIRGIN. FAVORED ART THOU...
I'M SORRY. DIDN'T CATCH THAT...
...YOU MIGHT WANT TO ANNUNCIATE BETTER

OKAY, YOU KNOW WHAT? I THINK I HAVE THE WRONG HOUSE.

i can see your house from here

i can see your house from here

OKAY, PEOPLE THAT WAS A JOKE! GEEZE!
HUH? WHAA?
NOTHING, SON. GO BACK TO SLEEP.

www.ingramcontent.com/pod-product-compliance
Lightning Source LLC
Chambersburg PA
CBHW081419090426
42738CB00017B/3420